BookRags Literature Study Guide

My Own Country: A Doctor's Story of a Town and Its People in the Age of AIDS by Abraham Verghese

Copyright Information

ISBN: 978-1-304-55669-1

Table of Contents

Plot Summary

In the summer of 1985, a young man driving from New York to Johnson City, Tennessee, becomes ill and is taken to the Johnson City Medical Center - known to staff as the Miracle Center - where a nurse, Claire Bellamy, realizes that his condition is serious and calls for help. Ray, a pulmonary doctor, soon comes to believe the young man has AIDS and the staff is horrified at the possibility of exposure. Abraham Verghese, author and internist, comes to Johnson City later where he hears about the young man - the city's only real case of AIDS. Abraham soon becomes the area specialist on AIDS and the related symptoms, drawing patients from around the region as AIDS becomes more prevalent in the area.

Abraham's first AIDS case is the brother of a young nurse named Essie. The young man, Gordon, has lived away from home for a long time and was already sick when he returned home. Essie immediately recognizes the ravages of the disease and calls on Abraham. After Gordon, Abraham begins seeing AIDS patients on a regular basis. These include Ed Maupin and Bobby Keller. They are gay and live together and both test positive for AIDS. Ed soon gives in to the disease and though Bobby urges that there be no heroic measures, Ed's brothers refuse to allow that, and Ed is on a ventilator for a short time before dying. Bobby lives for some time but dies before Abraham leaves Johnson City.

Abraham comes to realize that at least part of his discomfort is a fear that he doesn't have the roots that so many of his friends exhibit. Abraham also comes to realize that he is lacking the concrete faith in God exhibited by others, including a man named Will Johnson who was infected during a transfusion after a heart attack. Will declares a complete faith in God. As Abraham treats Will Johnson and his wife, Bess, who has also been infected, Abraham comes to realize that he has not been nearly as unbiased as he'd believed himself to be. Though Will could easily have become angry at the disease, he tells his son that no one - regardless of their sins - deserves this disease.

Abraham is soon the primary care physician for some fifty patients, and he begins to have problems on several fronts, not the least of which is the fact that his marriage is in trouble. By now Abraham has two sons and his wife, Rajani, feels that Abraham hasn't set his priorities so that his family takes an important role in his life. In fact, Abraham has come to the point that the constant struggle of dealing with the virus and its victims is weighing heavily on him. He eventually leaves Johnson City for a less stressful job in Iowa, hoping to give himself and his family a chance to recover.

Chapters One through Four Summary and Analysis

In the summer of 1985, a young man driving from New York to Johnson City, Tennessee, becomes ill and is taken to the Johnson City Medical Center - known to staff as the Miracle Center - where a nurse, Claire Bellamy, realizes that his condition is serious and calls for help. Ray, a pulmonary doctor, soon comes to believe the young man has AIDS and the staff is horrified at the possibility of exposure. The young man's parents come to the hospital as do two male friends from New York, and there's a tenuous peace between the man's family and friends. When he dies, there is concern over what to do with the ventilator but most put it down as having been a one-time situation because AIDS is a problem for the big cities, not for rural towns like Johnson City.

In chapter two, the author, Abraham Verghese, tells how he came to be in Johnson City. His parents are both from India and individually went to Ethiopia to teach physics where they met and married. Abraham began his studies, came to America and returned to India to complete his degree before returning to the United States. He interviews at several city hospitals but isn't comfortable with the "war zones" of the big cities, though he does meet and marry a girl named Rajani Chacko, also of Indian descent. He enters an intern program overseen by the East Tennessee State University, where he works at the Johnson City Medical Center and the Mountain Home Veterans Administration Medical Center. He also works weekends at several small, rural hospitals in the region where he learns about the culture. He learns that he likes most of the food and comes to understand the language - including that "roaches in the liver" is cirrhosis. He then spends two years in Boston but loses interest in medical research and returns to Boston.

Chapter three: Abraham and Rajani have the opportunity to return to Tennessee where Abraham is to work mainly at the V.A. hospital and to have some time for his research project - pneumonia in hamsters. Rajani is expecting their first child and they opt to take this opportunity over other big-city offers. They are to live on the V.A. campus in a large old house. Abraham talks about the people of the region as his reason for the choice, though the country is beautiful. Abraham is about to become a naturalized American citizen, and his son will be born American, and Abraham has finally found a country to call home.

In chapter four, Abraham describes some of the people he and Rajani come to know, including many of the V.A. patients who remain for awhile and then go to other states, migrating back with favorable weather. He also describes differences between the doctors and patients he sees at the V.A. and those he sees at the Miracle Center. Most V.A. patients are elderly men, but there is an array of patients at the Miracle Center.

Each Wednesday afternoon, Abraham sees patients at the University Physician's Group clinic and becomes known as the doctor to see for AIDS, though there have as yet been no cases. There he meets a student who has contracted genital warts, herpes and gonorrhea, and then a pastor who has gonorrhea, both which prompt Abraham to warn of AIDS, though both are negative. Abraham notes that no one outside the hospital knows about the previous case of AIDS. Abraham begins to talk more about AIDS, saying that it's like an iceberg with known cases above the water and the rest below the surface, as yet undiscovered. He then gives a talk to other physicians and notes that they are barely interested, having never seen a case of AIDS.

Then Abraham meets Olivia Sells with the local Red Cross. She asks him to go with her when she shows a video about AIDS and he agrees. She then sets up a date to show the video at a gay bar called The Connection. There follows a "flurry" of men coming into Abraham's Wednesday clinic for testing and none are positive, which makes Abraham hope that the virus hasn't reached rural Tennessee and he increases efforts at awareness.

--

The question about what to do with the ventilator used on Johnson City's first AIDS patient seems to be more than just a question of what's safe. The author notes that there are disinfecting techniques, but some want to get rid of the machine. The compromise is that many of the replaceable parts are replaced and the machine is disinfected multiple times, though it isn't used again for some time. The point seems to be that the ventilator was used to keep an AIDS patient alive, not that the disease might be spread. This seems typical of the stigma that accompanies AIDS in many situations.

Abraham notes that he knows nothing of the gay communities when AIDS first appears on the scene and soon discovers that there's an entire culture of which he hadn't been aware. Despite this, he's confident that medicine will soon understand and conquer AIDS. He says that only cancer is to be feared and that the only time cancer isn't cured is because there's some other problem - the patient is too old or didn't arrive soon enough for treatment - and never because the medicine failed.

Abraham admits that he fears his first trip to The Connection, not because he fears what might happen to him but because he thinks he might say or do something unacceptable in this situation. Abraham says that he later comes to the conclusion that being gay is a case of "nature over nurture," and that people who are gay are born that way. He bases this largely on the story of an AIDS victim he identifies only as James who says that he'd always felt more comfortable around his sisters and mother than around boys because he felt an attraction to boys and became easily flustered, just the same as most boys feel around young girls.

Chapters Five through Seven Summary and Analysis

In the fall of 1986 Abraham receives a message from Essie Vines. He'd known her during his first term working in the hospitals of rural Tennessee and Virginia. Essie is still working at that rural Virginia hospital and says that she's worried about her brother, Gordon, who has the HIV factor. Abraham tells Essie to meet him at the Miracle Center. Abraham warns the staff of Gordon's condition so they will take adequate precautions, noting that these are supposed to be standard procedures by now but aren't always followed.

Gordon tells Abraham that he had two lovers who died of AIDS and that he was probably infected in 1980 or 81. Abraham believes that Gordon is in the early stages of AIDS dementia and elects to keep him in the hospital. Essie backs Abraham's decision, though Gordon asks to go home. A few days later, Abraham travels to Essie's home on his way to an appointment to give a talk on AIDS. There he learns Gordon had had seizures as a child, dated as a teen and eventually moved away. Gordon had no communication with his family for several years, then called and told them he was living under a new identity as Brian Clark. They reconnected at Gordon's Florida home one Christmas. When Gordon showed up at the family home just days before Essie had called Abraham, it was obvious to her that he was sick but her family refused to acknowledge both the disease and its cause.

The following day, Abraham meets with Gordon's parents at the hospital where he announces that Gordon has AIDS. Gordon's father continues to believe that his son will recover. In the hospital, Abraham learns that there are only a few nurses willing to care for Gordon, as had been the case in Boston. One of those is Eleanor, who says a nurse named Mary is also willing. It's Eleanor who tells Abraham that there has been another AIDS victim at the hospital, though his diagnosis came late in his stay before he died at a rehabilitation center, having been put there for his drug addiction. Now Eleanor says that the AIDS patient is putting a strain on the nurses, pitting those who feel their duty is to care for all against those who refuse to care for AIDS patients.

In chapter six, Abraham sees an older, "prim and proper lady" he identifies only as Mrs. T. who shows him some "growths" she had taken from her pubic area. He discovers that it's actually crabs and provides medication. He learns that she got them from a lover and that she and her husband are no longer intimate, and then warns her about AIDS. Then Abraham learns that he's to see Ed Maupin and Bobby Keller together, both wanting an AIDS test. They've driven from Abdington, Virginia, to see Abraham, fearing the problems that would arise if word got around in their small town that they were even tested. They say that there is no "significant" gay population in Abdington, that both had been married and fathered children before admitting they were gay and moving in together. They also admit to going to a truck stop for sex, that they never use a condom and that they don't charge for sex.

Abraham checks in regularly on Gordon and tries to find the source of a recurring fever, though he will later discover that an unexplained recurring fever isn't at all uncommon in AIDS patients. One day Gordon declares that he's seen a vision of Jesus and his attitude changes. His mother is in the room at the time and says she detected an "aura," though did not witness Abraham's vision. Gordon's fever drops to near normal and Abraham seizes the opportunity to send him home, noting that Gordon plans to be baptized immediately.

Abraham gets the test results back for Ed and Bobby and both are infected. That same day, he has an appointment with Fred Goodson and Otis Jackson, also gay and both having already tested positive for HIV. Fred is very informed and says he doesn't believe Otis infected him.

In chapter seven, a man named Clyde McCray and it treated by a series of specialists who cannot find the cause of his illness until one doctor orders a blood test and discovers that Clyde is HIV positive. His wife Vickie, a large woman who always wears a bandana, is devastated, drives to their trailer and gets a gun. She plans to kill Clyde, then their two children and then herself, but can't bring herself to do so. When Abraham sees Clyde the first time, Clyde admits to having had sex with men, the unabashed admission an apparent result of the AIDS dementia itself. Vickie is angry and Clyde pulls the sheet up over his head, hiding in a very childlike manner.

At the Wednesday clinic, Abraham gives the news to Bobby and Ed.

Bobby cries, saying that he is worried about Ed who has been tired for some time. Abraham warns them about unsafe sex practices but notes that he isn't certain they'll be careful. Abraham them calls Fred and Otis with news of their blood tests, results that indicate Fred is already in danger. Vickie calls that afternoon and Abraham goes to sit with her in a hospital quiet room where she talks about her life. She says that she'd always felt Clyde was "oversexed," that he'd had an affair with her sister and that she would have left him except that she had nowhere to go unless she returned to the home of an abusive father. Abraham notes that he's drawn Vickie's blood but believes Clyde might have been so busy sleeping around that he hadn't infected her. That's not the case and both Vickie and her sister are positive for HIV but none of the children are. The family's life changes dramatically as Clyde spends most of his time playing cars with his young son, Vickie becomes the sole breadwinner and their daughter helps care for the family.

--

When Abraham tells Rajani that he is about to see his first AIDS patient in Tennessee, he can't hide his excitement. Rajani never fully understands Abraham's dedication to this field and he admits that it probably sounds strange to others that he would be so enthralled with the AIDS patients. His interest goes beyond the disease to the lifestyle which will also garner some problems at home, though his interest seems to be merely a way to learn more about the habits of those prone to contract the disease. Abraham notes that he prefers not to see Rajani's fear and that he doesn't yet know how the AIDS virus will take over his own life. From that statement, it sounds as if he might be hinting that he later becomes infected though this isn't the case.

Abraham notes that the fact that he's foreign may actually be a positive point when he's dealing with AIDS victims. He says that he believes some people are more comfortable talking to him about their sexual encounters and possible points of contracting the virus because he isn't like the person next door. He also seems to work very hard at maintaining a nonjudgmental attitude which some other doctors don't do.

Abraham takes extensive histories from his patients and says that there are two reasons for it. The first is that he wants to know his patients as people. The second is that he is working to compile information about the practices of his patients and their symptoms and disease progression. One night Rajani asks Abraham about his apparent fascination with the gay lifestyle and whether he's attracted to the gay men he encounters. He tries to explain it scientifically, including his impression that gay men have the ability to be what they want without worrying what women and society expect of them. He says that the number and variety of partners of the gay men are examples of what all men would have, except that women forbid it. Abraham says that he's satisfied with his explanation but Rajani is apparently not, and walks away from him. He calls out after her that he's not attracted, but the answer may have been too late for his wife's peace of mind.

Chapters Seven through Thirteen Summary and Analysis

One Wednesday, Gordon arrives at the clinic and Abraham is shocked at how much trouble he's having breathing. His father refuses to believe there's anything really wrong with Gordon, even now, and Abraham calls Essie. She says that Gordon has decided that he wants to die at home. Abraham reluctantly allows him to leave. A couple nights later, Gordon is taken to their local emergency room and the doctor determines that Gordon has had a stroke. Essie says that if Abraham can do something for Gordon in the hospital, she'll bring him there, but that she otherwise wants to relieve his suffering as much as possible and take him home. He dies five days later and Essie has to call in a mortician other than the one the family always uses because of the fear of AIDS. She relates this fact to Abraham, saying that they'd had a closed casket but that she'd ordered it opened to make certain Gordon had on socks. When she found his bare feet, she ordered the squeamish mortician to put socks on him and the man had tried to accomplish the task with heavy gloves. Abraham doesn't attend the funeral but goes with Essie a few days later to visit Gordon's grave. Essie tells him that her site is just to the left of Gordon's.

In chapter nine, Abraham wakes to find Rajani - now in her ninth month of pregnancy with their second son - asleep on a mound of pillows and their two-year-old son, Steven, asleep beside them. Now, in 1987 and a few months after the death of Gordon, Abraham's list of AIDS patients is in the "double digits." Abraham's days are busy, including his work at the V.A., his research on hamsters, and his rounds at the hospital. On this particular day, he checks in on Scotty Daws, a young man who had come to the emergency room and been admitted for pneumonia. He was found to be HIV positive. When his condition worsened, a sister and uncle were summoned. Neither seemed to realize or care what was happening to Scotty, and Abraham made the decision to put him on a respirator. Now Scotty continues to live on the machine with no hope of recovery and Abraham faces an impossible position - nurses hate caring for the hopeless case and Abraham doesn't believe it would be ethical to remove the respirator at this point. He places a "do not resuscitate" order and goes to his lab where he and Betty Franzus, a research technician, perform the day's duties on the hamsters.

Abraham next goes to the V.A. for rounds and notes that the personal aspect is preferable to the more sterile surroundings at the Miracle Center. He has treated two V.A. patients infected by AIDS and admits that the disease is quickly taking most of his focus. He says that he wants someone to proclaim the danger more strenuously and worries about how many cases are undiagnosed. At the end of this particular day, he goes home some twelve hours after his day began, determined to play with Steven and forget AIDS for awhile. Abraham's parents are visiting to help with the new baby. After dinner, Rajani tells Abraham that the baby has stopped moving, and they rush to the hospital where the eventual outcome is a healthy baby boy they name Jacob George Verghese, Jacob for Rajani's father and George for Abraham's.

In chapter ten, Abraham talks of the changes that come following the birth of Jacob. Abraham and Steven spend evenings together and one evening Abraham gets a message that Scotty Daws has "coded." He rushes to the hospital and stops an attempt to resuscitate that a nurse initiated despite the order. Abraham then learns of an AIDS support group call TAP that has become active. Abraham attends a meeting and learns a great deal about the various members, their lifestyles, discoveries of being gay and background. He is late getting home and discovers their babysitter's car outside and Rajani all dressed up, only then remembering that he had promised to be home early because they'd been invited out for dinner.

In chapter eleven, Abraham and Rajani attend a party at the Ashley Academy gym - a trend that has recently prompted a series of similar parties. Here they encounter an array of people, including the "techies" from Eastman-Kodak and doctors. Abraham notes that there is a definite hierarchy that puts an enormous amount of emphasis on wealth. When he is ready to leave, he sees Rajani surrounded by friends and finds himself reluctant to urge her to leave early.

In chapter twelve, Abraham goes to visit Clyde and Vickie McCray at their home in Tester Hollow. They live on McCray Road in a trailer with an addition that forms a "T." Clyde is asleep when Abraham arrives and doesn't wake during the visit. Vickie takes Abraham for a tour of the house and tells about her life. She notes that Clyde sometimes wanders off, usually catching a ride to the home of his mother, a cousin or to his "favorite watering hole." When Vickie goes to bring him home, he's sometimes petulant. Vickie says that Clyde had stated one morning that he was going to "just go around and give this to as many people as I can." Vickie says that he rationalized this thought with the argument that someone had infected him. Vickie says she threatened Clyde's life and he hasn't mentioned it again.

Abraham turns the conversation to Jewell, an older man who Clyde claims had been his lover. Vickie says that the two had gone off together occasionally and that she'd never suspected a sexual relationship. She says that Jewell had loaned the family money at various times, that he'd given Vickie three hundred dollars recently, and that she believes she can count on him for support more than her own family.

In chapter thirteen, Bobby Keller calls to say that Ed is very ill and Abraham agrees to meet them at the emergency room. There, he realizes from Ed's appearance that he is in trouble, and Bobby immediately insists that Ed not be put on life-support machines. However, Bobby has nothing in writing and Ed's family - including his older brother - veto that decision and tell Abraham to do everything they can to help Ed beat the pneumonia. Abraham notes that he could have negated the decision if he had told them there was no hope for Ed, but he tells them that there's a good chance Ed can recover from the pneumonia he's currently fighting and could have some more time. Ed is put on a ventilator and moved to the intensive care unit. Abraham is called from the hospital the following morning at four thirty with the news that Ed has stopped breathing and that resuscitation efforts have been undergoing for five minutes. He tells them to call Ed's "lover and family" and to continue their efforts. When he arrives, Ed remains unresponsive and Abraham orders them to stop, has a brief encounter with an angry nurse, then goes to tell the family.

--

Gordon's father's attitude is probably typical of some families. His father refuses to acknowledge that Gordon's illness is serious and when Gordon dies, his father tells people that Gordon died of a stroke. He ignores the source of the stroke even after being pushed into facing it. Gordon's mother seems to know about her son's lifestyle but is also unwilling to admit it out loud. This is the same kind of attitude seen in the parents of Johnson City's very first AIDS case.

Betty Franzus, Abraham's research assistant, obviously has a sense of humor. Betty seems to be carrying on a great deal of the research. She medicates the hamsters, then Abraham puts a tube into their lungs and introduces a bacteria, then massages them into breathing again. When there's a "hamster Code Blue," they use a tiny ventilator until the hamster recovers. The hamsters, breathing normally, are then given back to Betty who puts them into a separate cage marked, "recovery, immediate family only."

As Abraham prepares to leave the McCray home, he urges Vickie to consider attending a meeting of the support group. She seems reluctant but promises to think about it. This is an example of the different ways people have of dealing with the situation. Some, such as Fred, have become proponents of rights and education and others, like Otis, have simply given up. There will soon be another victim introduced who depends solely on his faith in Jesus.

When only one nurse remains in the room, Abraham says that he'd thought he could help Ed rally so that he could have a few more months or even years of life. The nurse says she doesn't understand the point of trying because all AIDS patients are going to die anyway. Abraham is furious and says he wants to ask what she'd want if she were in that situation - to just be allowed to die or for someone to try to give her some more time. He says that he also wants to point out that everyone is going to die someday which means - by her line of reasoning - that they should only provide care for immortals. He doesn't respond aloud at all, telling himself that he needs to "choose his battles."

Chapters Fourteen through Nineteen Summary and Analysis

Abraham notes that he feels a deep longing and that it could be a longing for home, though he doesn't know what home really is. He also seems to worry that it could be a forewarning of death. In chapter fifteen, Abraham receives a phone call from Dr. Sarah Presnell who tells of a couple, Will and Bess Johnson, who have HIV after Will received a blood transfusion. Will suffered a heart attack that prompted a seizure following the funeral of a good friend. He was taken to Duke University where he underwent surgery. Will was discharged and it was later discovered that he had two broken vertebrae - apparently the result of his thrashing around during the seizure.The Johnsons insist on confidentiality, including having a different diagnosis on their insurance forms, and Abraham agrees to meet them at the hospital. He helps the Johnsons check in after their two-hour drive to reach the hospital. Will is now suffering from a severe sore throat caused by lesions that have not responded to any medications. Abraham prescribes medications. Later, at home with Rajani, she admits that she wishes that Abraham had not become so engrossed in the treatment of AIDS but realizes that the disease isn't going to go away.

In chapter sixteen, Will notes that the gastroenterologist who saw him the previous day seemed uncomfortable and that this was the first hospital employee here who he'd believed felt this way. Abraham notes that the doctor never returns to see the Johnsons for a follow-up visit. Later that day, Abraham meets with the father of AIDS patient B.J. Hilton. With B.J.'s permission, Abraham tells B.J.'s father what to expect as the illness runs its course. He then examines a young gay man he'd met at The Connection named Raleigh, who plays the part of the Southern Belle and refuses to be serious. Next, Abraham examines Bess Johnson, who is largely asymptomatic; she tells about her life and her marriage. She relates that a young intern had told her that Will had received a significant amount of blood and that she should remember this if Will had health problems later, but that she hadn't really understood and that no one had mentioned the possibility of AIDS from a transfusion.

The next morning, Abraham learns that Raleigh had "taken an overdose of sleeping pills" after his visit, but had survived. The news makes it clear to Abraham that treating the symptoms isn't the end of his duties to his patients and he feels the weight of responsibility for being the sole care provider for these people. He relates that to large hospitals where a team of doctors were each responsible for only one aspect of care.

In chapter seventeen, Abraham continues to treat patients seven years after the AIDS epidemic began, though he remains without any significant treatment options. Abraham compares the AIDS activists in the larger cities to the patients he sees who remain largely in hiding. He now has about fifty patients and provides all the care for each of them, as opposed to the large hospitals where, as one doctor put it, the "drones" do all the clinic work.

Abraham then sees a new patient, Petie Granger, who had recently returned from Baltimore to his parents' home. After a week, Petie is beginning to show improvement from his recent bout with pneumonia and his mother takes him to her personal physician - an man they've known as doctor and friend for many years. The doctor refuses to see Petie, as do a series of other doctors--until they locate Abraham. As Abraham remains frustrated with the lack of treatment options, he buys a series of magazines that report on potential treatments. Had he been in a larger city, he would likely have known about treatment trials but feels cut off from his remote location.

Abraham has known about Will's faith in God, but one day Will tells Abraham that he has ultimate faith in God and that he knows he won't be asked to handle more than he can. Abraham is tearful when he leaves the room and wonders if this difference in faith is what makes Abraham's life so different from that of Will. He says that his own belief in God is abstract, but what Will describes is concrete. The next day, Will describes a vision he's had of Jesus. Abraham then tells Will about a study Duke is conducting with a new drug for AIDS and Will agrees to participate only if Abraham writes to Duke because Will has told Duke of his contracting the AIDS virus there and was ignored. Will and Bess are accepted into the program and their care is turned over to Duke. Abraham notes that he soon has the ability to prescribe a new drug called AZT that benefits some, though is very expensive. He says that he feels "empowered" because he finally is able to do something.

In chapter eighteen, Abraham hears from a dentist who unknowingly treated an AIDS patient. Though he took normal precautions, he was angry that he didn't know and says a druggist - who filled the man's AIDS prescriptions - called him with the information when the patient took a prescription from the dentist to be filled. Abraham is angry at the druggist for betraying a confidence but the man, Ethan Nidiffer, tells Abraham that he'd called every dentist in the region, given no name but says that he is HIV infected, and everyone refused to see him. Abraham is angry at the situation, including the fact that AIDS has come to be associated overtly with gays but admits that this public perception is mainly because those who are not outlandish in action and dress prefer to remain anonymous. The druggist - a man Abraham had sent a great deal of business to in the past - calls Abraham to defend himself, and Abraham decides he won't send any more patients there.

In chapter nineteen, Abraham sees the emerging personalities and relationships of those involved in the AIDS support group. Ethan, older than most, somewhat reserved and intolerant of those he calls "flaming queers," becomes the counterpart to Bobby Keller, the one who always has a retort. Petie Granger wants everyone to remain optimistic and upbeat and Fred Goodson tries to keep meetings on track. Vickie and Clyde attend with Vickie spending some of the time with the AIDS victims and some of the time with the families who provide support. Abraham spends a particular morning with lung cancer victims and says that the afternoon with AIDS patients is "positively uplifting."

--

Will and Bess refuse to tell anyone of their health problems, including their children, believing that the stigma associated with AIDS will come to haunt them though they became infected through a hospital error rather than any fault of their own. Will also believes that the information could damage the reputation of his company and that they will be ostracized from their church and social circle. They refuse to consider sharing the information. Abraham's attitude toward the Johnson's is interesting and he admits that he treats them differently because they are the "innocent" victims of the disease. He questions his attitude, reasoning that he must then consider the gay men who contracted the disease "guilty."

It's apparent that Abraham's marriage is suffering, but Abraham himself has become associated with AIDS patients to the point that he feels he is constantly under fire. This alienation is wearing on him and seems to be drifting over into other parts of his life, evidenced by his lack of tolerance for fears and biases of all kinds.

Chapters Twenty through Twenty-Six Summary and Analysis

Abraham has a patient named Cameron Tolliver, an AIDS patient who is in serious pain. Abraham talks of his worry over calling in surgeons, admitting that they are at greater risk in the operating room than he with routine examinations. He says that he tries to call on each of the available surgeons equally. One young surgeon balks until his "crusty" counterpart orders the young surgeon to do his duty with the threat that he - the older man - would do it for him. The young surgeon gives in. In Cameron's case, a woman named Sue McCoy is to be the surgeon and she agrees to have Abraham in the operating room, later confiding that she is always fearful when doing surgery on AIDS patients.

In chapter twenty-one, Abraham describes Norman Sanger, a young hemophiliac who says that as a child he would stay awake at night in excruciating pain so that his parents might have a good night's sleep. He grew up in California and moved to Kentucky to attend college, staying because of the excellent care available for hemophiliacs. He knows he is HIV positive two years before seeing Abraham, though Abraham is aware of him for some time prior to that. Norman met Claire, a young widow with a small son and married her shortly after discovering his HIV status, and Claire, who has had a difficult life, stands by Norman despite his illnesses. Norman responds positively to the AZT treatment but then comes down with pneumonia, and Abraham notes that one night on the phone Norman, now in the hospital, seems depressed. Abraham goes to visit him and Norman says that, more than anything, he fears that he can't remain courageous and dignified - traits that have been vital to him throughout his life. Abraham cries as he leaves.

In chapter twenty-two, Abraham visits with Vickie McCray and learns that Clyde threw a fit to go to Nashville to the Grand Ole Opry and the Knoxville Zoo. Vickie refuses and Clyde runs away. She finally catches up with him and eventually gives in to both demands. After the trips, Clyde lies down and seems to have given up his will to live. Vickie says that she has become close friends with Bobby Keller and a man known as "Jacko," though she says she's surprised. Bobby has shown a caring side and the three of them cared for Cameron during his final days of life. In chapter twenty-three, Clyde fades quickly and Vickie insists on keeping him at home. With the help of hospice she does so. Vickie and Danielle are with Clyde when he dies. Abraham notes that death is the end each of the AIDS patients will face and that he wants to run away from it.

In chapter twenty-four, Will Johnson Junior, son of Will and Bess, puts clues together and comes to believe his father has AIDS. Will and Bess send Will Junior and his sister a copy of the journals they have kept since the diagnosis confirming the fears. The entries detail their reactions, their reasons for keeping the information secret and the understanding that their son and daughter now have the option to take whatever precautions they feel necessary.

In chapter twenty-five, Abraham learns that Norman Sanger has died of bleeding. Abraham contacts Norman's close friend and coworker, Sharon Phillips, months later to learn about Norman's final moments of life. She tells him that Norman had begun bleeding profusely, probably from a lung hemorrhage, and that for some reason he called for an ambulance. Sharon says the four of them spent an evening together on the Fourth of July and that Norman said he wanted them to rent a chalet together. Though they all know he is dying and the plan couldn't come to fruition, they all agree and he later tells Sharon that he's made a reservation at a chalet called Heaven's Gate. Sharon and Claire are with Norman at the hospital and then together later at home where Sharon tells Claire that Norman is now at "Heaven's Gate."

--

Abraham describes an odor he smells as he enters the rooms of both Cameron Tolliver and Norman Sanger and says that he comes to associate that odor always with AIDS. When he arrives home one night, he showers hurriedly and hopes his family doesn't detect the odor and or associate that odor with Abraham. It seems that Norman's faltering fear affects Abraham more than it should and it seems this is a sign that Abraham is burning out. He has taken on a monumental task and is simply becoming tired from the burden he carries. He also sees his weakness as unacceptable and worries about its impact on his patients more than its impact on himself.

Abraham notes that the deathbed is the place where he is most uncomfortable and he never knows what to do. Though he is not alone in this among his colleagues, he resolves after hearing of Norman's final moments to do better. He notes that Norman had probably panicked at the horror of his lungs filling up with blood and had therefore ended his life in chaos with an ambulance ride and the heroics of the medical staff trying to save him. Abraham says that, had he been there, he would have treated Norman with large doses of morphine because that allows the mind to disconnect from the horror of what's happening with the body. He then resolves that he will never be without morphine at a deathbed and that he will be a larger presence for his dying patients. While his resolve is a good thing for his patients, it's bound to be taking a larger toll on Abraham and his family.

Chapters Twenty-Seven through Thirty-One Summary and Analysis

A man Abraham had seen two years earlier, Luther Hines, reappears at the clinic. He's in terrible shape, has stopped taking most of his medications, lives alone without friends or family, and refuses to be put in the hospital or to attend the local AIDS support group. Abraham reluctantly provides a refill on a prescription and lets him leave. Then Abraham learns that Otis has died in Fred's arms. Fred has been provided morphine and administers it freely. Abraham notes the difference between Fred's death and that of Norman. Fred notes that Otis had been angry until he confided in Fred his desire for baptism. When Fred tells him that the repentance is vital but that the baptism is secondary, Otis seems more at peace. Fred says that he felt accepted by Otis' family, especially one aunt who lived very simply without electricity, but that the preacher had remarked on the fact that people bring things on themselves.

In chapter twenty-seven, Abraham meets with Will Junior and it's noted that he envies Will Junior's self-assurance. Abraham seems to associate that with Junior's roots and his own lack of self-assurance with his own lack of a place where he feels at home. They talk about several topics, including the fact that foreign doctors are flocking to America. Abraham points out that India has enough doctors but none have money to provide even the most basic care. Junior says that his father has continued to fight but remains adamant that the virus is Satan's work, and that he has seen visions of Satan on several occasions.

In chapter twenty-eight, Hobart Carter is another of Abraham's patients. When Hobart's father tells Abraham that Hobart is "fading fast," Abraham prescribes morphine and, upon learning of Hobart's death, goes to the apartment where Hobart lives with his parents.

In chapter twenty-nine, Vickie McCray and other members of the AIDS support group decide to call Petie Granger and other members of the group who aren't in attendance during a meeting just before Thanksgiving. The woman who answers the phone says that Petie died two days earlier and that the funeral has already taken place. A short time later, Abraham learns that Will Johnson died, followed soon by Bess. Meanwhile Vickie, while realistic that the AIDS will eventually manifest and her life end, remains active and positive and has enrolled in nursing school.

In chapter thirty, Bobby Keller has died while Luther Hines, looking more horrible by the moment and blaming everyone around him for failure to adequately treat his symptoms, remains in the hospital. One day, Abraham and a group of interns visit Luther's room where Abraham goes through the motions of examining him though there's nothing more to be done for him.

In chapter thirty-one, the date is December 31, 1989, and Abraham packs the last of his items in his lab. He is planning to go to Iowa where he won't be responsible as primary care physician but will be part of an AIDS team. He describes it as a "cooling-off period," and he and his family set out on their journey to their new home. As they near their new home, Abraham's thoughts drift back to a young man who had driven into Johnson City years earlier, the first case of confirmed AIDS in the city. He says that he believes a man who arrives in the same situation now would find better care and a more open-minded community. Abraham says that he believes this to be true because he has faith in the town and its people.

--

Abraham spends some time mapping where all his current AIDS victims live now and where they likely contracted the virus, and discovers that most contracted it along the coasts or near Chicago, though there are a few that don't fit the profile, probably having gotten the disease from truck stops of some other unprotected chance sexual encounter.

Rajani asks Abraham to go with him to a marriage counselor. Abraham sees it as an impossible situation. He says that the problem is that he hasn't enough time and that taking time out for a counselor isn't going to change that. Rajani is angry that Abraham has time for his patients and makes time for tennis and friends but not for his family.

Important People

Abraham Verghese

The author and a doctor specializing in infectious diseases who arrives at the Johnson City Medical Center soon after the first case of AIDS had been treated there. Abraham is from Africa, studied in India, and arrived in the United States in 1980 as a "rookie doctor." While he knows there are some aspects of medicine that are more glamorous and some doctors that earn more money, he enters into the field of infectious diseases. One of his motivations is that there is little competition for the positions in this field. While he doesn't realize it at the time, he and other specialists of this field will become in high demand as the AIDS epidemic becomes a major problem. Abraham begins to study up on AIDS but from his new home in Tennessee, sees no cases.

After some time, the brother of a nurse in another small hospital becomes Abraham's first AIDS patient. He is excited as he waits for this first consultation and that excitement continues as he sees new patients, each with an array of symptoms to treat. The excitement soon wanes as Abraham feels the stress of watching helplessly as his patients die, one after another. He admits to finding comfort in the routine of examinations while a patient is on his deathbed and there's really nothing Abraham can do. Then there are some studies and a new drug treatment, though the impact of the drug remains limited. Eventually, the stress of his practice - which earns him precious little money and takes an enormous amount of time and physical and emotional strength - takes its toll on Abraham, his family, his marriage and his own peace of mind. Feeling that he has no other option, he takes on a new job in Iowa and prepares to become part of an AIDS team.

Vickie McCray

One of the first to be diagnosed with AIDS under Abraham's care and one of only two women he describes in any detail, Vickie McCray is the wife of Clyde McCray. Clyde is diagnosed first and freely admits to having had unprotected sex with other men. He also had an affair with Vickie's sister and infected both Vickie and her sister with the virus. Vickie is a large woman, and her life seems very limited before Clyde contracted the virus. After the diagnosis, Abraham urges Vickie to seek out the support of a local AIDS support group. Though she is initially skeptical, she later becomes an activist for the cause.

Long after her diagnosis, she tells Abraham that in many ways her life is now better than before the virus became a constant threat of full-blown AIDS. Vickie's strength is amazing and she stands by Clyde, keeping him at home and caring for him until his death. She then enrolls in nursing school and admits that her best friends are two gay men, both infected with AIDS. Though she is holding out hope for a future for herself, she has also admitted to the reality that she will likely become an AIDS victim and makes arrangements for her children's future after her own death.

Rajani Chacko

The wife of the author, she is an executive for an advertising agency when they marry and move to Tennessee. Rajani is often angry at the long hours Abraham spends with his patients and fears the possibility of spreading the virus to their sons, though Abraham assures her this is not possible. When Rajani suggests counseling, Abraham objects, noting that a counselor could not possibly instruct him on how to make more time for his family.

Gordon Vines

A brother of a hospital employee, Gordon is the first AIDS patient to be solely in Abraham's care. Abraham notes that he spends a great deal of time and energy trying to figure out what causes Gordon's fever, but that he would later learn that fever of this kind was typical of AIDS victims. Gordon is also the first to die under Abraham's care.

Ed Maupin

Ed is one of Abraham's first AIDS patients and among the first to die under Abraham's care. When Ed becomes very ill and is taken to the emergency room, his lover, Bobby Keller, tells Abraham that Ed did not want to be placed on a ventilator to sustain his life. Abraham learns that Ed did not put this in writing nor did he give Bobby power of attorney, and so turns to Ed's brothers for a decision. Ed's life is sustained only briefly on machines.

Bobby Keller

Bobby is the gay lover of Ed Maupin. He is a happy person who tends to joke a lot, a fact that gets on the nerves of some of his counterparts. He becomes very active in the AIDS support group and close friends with several there. Bobby and Abraham are always somewhat reserved with each other after Ed's death because Abraham had observed the rights of Ed's brother's to have Ed put on a ventilator rather than Bobby's assurance that Ed did not want these measures.

Ethan Nidiffer

A young man who becomes one of Abraham's patients, Ethan finds himself in need of a dentist but can find no one who will see him when he tells them he has AIDS. He finally hides his AIDS status and sees a dentist who prescribes medication after the procedure. When Ethan has his prescription filled at the same pharmacy where he has his AIDS medications filled, the druggist takes it upon himself to tell the dentist of Ethan's AIDS. Ethan seems less upset by the situation than Abraham who initially wants to chastise Ethan but then sees his quandary.

Will Johnson

A man who is infected with the AIDS virus during a transfusion following heart surgery. Will and his wife, Bess, are pillars of the community and church and have an active social circle. At the advice of their physician and fearing the reactions of others, they decide to keep their disease a secret and don't share the information until their son, Will Junior, deduces what's wrong.

Clyde McCray

Clyde is the husband of Vickie McCray and freely admits in the hospital to Abraham that he had engaged in unprotected sex with a man. When the illness takes a serious toll on Clyde, resulting in dementia, he runs away from home, demanding that he have the opportunity to see the Grand Ole Opry. When he's made that trip and a trip to the Knoxville Zoo, he seems to give up hope and soon dies at home in the arms of his wife and daughter.

Norman Sanger

The young hemophiliac who has contracted AIDS from blood transfusions. Norman is a strong individual who describes a childhood of staying awake at night in excruciating pain until morning so that his parents have a good night's sleep. Norman falls in love with a young widow and they marry, though he has already been diagnosed with AIDS. As the disease becomes more debilitating, he fears the loss of his own strength and courage and, when a hemorrhage causes his lungs to fill with blood, panics and calls for an ambulance so that his final moments are in a hospital and chaotic. Abraham learns from Norman and vows always to use drugs to cushion the fear of a patient on his deathbed.

Objects/Places

Johnson City Medical Center

The hospital in Tennessee where the young man dies of AIDS and where the author, Abraham Verghese, returns to work as a doctor specializing in infectious diseases.

India

Where Abraham Verghese completes medical school.

Boston City Hospital

Where Abraham Verghese is offered a position prior to his work in Tennessee.

The Connection

A gay bar in Johnson City where Abraham goes with a Red Cross representative to show a video about AIDS.

Rural Virginia

Where the hospital is located where Essie Vines works.

Abdington, Virginia

Where Ed Maupin and Bobby Keller live.

Blackwood

Where Essie and Gordon live with their family.

Tester Hollow

Where Clyde and Vickie McCray live.

Duke University Hospital

Where Will Johnson was given AIDS-infected blood and where he is later involved in a study of a possible treatment.

Johnson City, Tennessee

Where Abraham and his family live and where he works at the hospital and V.A. Center

Themes

The Need for a Home

The title of the book is indicative of the author's own longing to belong somewhere, and he frequently mentions the fact that he is envious of those who have roots. Though this longing is often at the heart of Abraham's thoughts, he also despises the "clannish" tendencies of some of his friends who are also from India. On at least one occasion, Abraham seems to wonder if this longing is not so much for a place, as for something else, and he seems interested in the very concrete faith described by Will Johnson. It seems that Rajani is also seeking this as she undertakes to buy a house, though Abraham is less than enthusiastic about the endeavor. She wants that stability to be in Tennessee, but Abraham's level of burnout seems to be so high that he cannot abide the idea of home being here.

Abraham is not the only person to feel this need as evidenced by the map he creates one evening depicting the places where his current AIDS patients live as opposed to where they lived when they became infected. Many of them were residents of the area who moved away to other places - usually big cities - where they could be themselves without hiding their sexuality. Now these men are returning home, to the place they were born and raised and where they will be with family as their inevitable deaths approach. This tendency takes place even for those who find themselves unwelcome by family and friends, indicating their ties to the memories of this place to be an apparent symbol of home.

The Stigma of AIDS

Several of the patients treated by AIDS did not become infected through unprotected homosexual sex, though the majority of them were gay men. Abraham notes that the activists in the larger cities are mainly openly and flamboyantly gay, which soon creates a public perception that only gay men are infected with the virus. There are those who are angry at the perception, but Abraham seems to understand that those who speak out put a face on the disease while many of his patients in rural Tennessee - patients who are often more conservative or not gay at all - remain quiet. He notes that the fact that others refuse to speak out means that the public has only one kind of person to associate with the disease and that person happens to be openly gay. This public perception prompts some to hide their illness. An extreme case of this is Will and Bess Johnson who refuse to tell even their children the truth of the disease, fearing that the stigma will cause them to be ostracized. This turns out to be untrue, but the perception of the stigma was sufficient to worry the Johnsons. It should be noted that the stigma stretched to the medical community as evidenced by the dentists and doctors who outright refused to take on AIDS patients at all.

The Weight of Responsibility

Abraham chooses infectious diseases as his field of specialty without realizing that the AIDS virus will make men in his field in high demand. As he begins his work on AIDS, he is excited and conveys that excitement to his wife. He spends a great deal of time with his first patient, Gordon, searching for ways to make Gordon more comfortable and treating the various symptoms. It should be noted that Abraham has encountered AIDS before, but Gordon is the first patient to be solely in Abraham's care. This may have been exciting to Abraham in the beginning, but he is soon seeing some fifty AIDS patients, each with a unique set of problems. Moreover, Abraham tries to learn as much about the patient personally as possible, mostly in an effort to learn more about this virus but also because he wants to help the individuals and their families. Then a young man named Raleigh attempts suicide soon after a visit to Abraham's office and Abraham feels the full weight of this responsibility. It's a weight that eventually pushes Abraham out of the clinic he's working in and into a team environment, a situation he calls a "cooling off period" from the responsibility of being sole medical provider for such a needy group.

Style

Perspective

The story is written in first-person from the perspective of the author, Abraham Verghese. This is the only real option available. Had the author chosen a third-person point of view, the result would likely have been clinical and devoid of emotion. As it is, the author's torment, feelings and fears become a vital part of the story. The use of this first person doesn't greatly limit the story as in many first-person stories because the author is the only link to many of these people and because he seeks out and relates details that would not otherwise be part of his first-hand knowledge. Through this method, the reader is provided sufficient information to be fully informed about the people and events discussed in this story.

Tone

The tone of the story is predominantly sad and depressing, as is to be expected in a story on this topic. Readers must understand that there are no "magic cures" for the AIDS virus and that at the time of the story, there were many unknown factors that contributed to even earlier deaths. The people who tested positive for AIDS were doomed to an early - and often undignified and painful - death. In addition, the weight of responsibility on Abraham as the sole provider of medical care for many of these people is a constant drain on his emotional well-being. This makes the story even more dark and foreboding. There are, however, points of light and hope throughout the story. Though Will Johnson dies, he does so proclaiming his love and trust in Jesus. Though Vickie McCray has the HIV virus, she makes plans to go to nursing school and says that her life is fuller than it had been before she learned that each day is a gift to be savored. It should be noted that there are portions of the book that contain graphic details of the illness, the symptoms and the manifestations. These occur only occasionally but some readers may find them disturbing.

Structure

The book is divided into thirty-one chapters of varying length. Chapters may be as brief as four pages while other range to more than twenty pages. The book is presented roughly in chronological fashion with one exception. The first chapter presents the arrival of the first known AIDS victims to Johnson City, Tennessee, then drops back to tell the story of Abraham Verghese and his arrival in the country as an infectious diseases physician. Some of the chapters cover one event or series of events. For example, chapter thirteen covers Ed Maupin's sudden onset of pneumonia and the events leading up to his death. Other chapters are not so clear-cut in their beginnings and endings. For example, chapter fifteen covers the arrival of Will Johnson as one of Abraham's patients and the majority of that chapter dwells on the story of Will and Bess. Chapter sixteen begins with Will Johnson, saying that his illness had not improved over a particular night, then skips to another of Abraham's patients, Raleigh, then to Bess Johnson, back to Will and then back to Raleigh. There is a theme to the chapter - that Abraham is feeling the need to provide more than just medication and feels the weight of responsibility of being primary physician for AIDS patients.

Quotes

"Everyone thought it had been a freak accident, a one-time thing in Johnson City. This was a small town in the country, a town of clean-living, good country people. AIDS was clearly a big city problem. It was something that happened in other kinds of lives." Chapter 1, Page 13

"On the matter of how my parents met, how they courted, I dare not ask my father. Any my mother, though seemingly willing, parts with no significant details. My brothers and I always thought it had something to do with physics." Chapter 2, Page 16

"For the Indian parties, Rajani wore a sari and we completely immersed ourselves in a familiar and affectionate culture in which we had our definite place as the juniormost couple; but at night we could don jeans and boots and go line dancing at the Sea Horse on West Walnut or listen to blues at the Down Home." Chapter 2, Page 23

"I realize now that Rajani was scarcely inscrutable at this moment in our marriage - she was merely frightened, as any wife or mother would be, as so many were in the days when we understood so little about AIDS. For my sake, she swallowed her fear, said nothing when she realized that the sound in my voice was excitement, exhilaration." Chapter 5, Page 75

"'Safe sex' was a cerebral concept that sounded good in my office. Yet, it was not the cerebrum, but some other part of the body that took over when a good-looking man cruised them in the grocery store and beckoned for them to follow in the direction of his car. Of course, this was far from a problem confined to gay men: No cerebral abstraction involving sex - whether it was the need for contraception, proscriptions against adultery, or the need for safe sex - had ever in human history fared well in the face of raw lust." Chapter 7, Page 133

"Among the men, the pecking order at these functions was clear: doctors ruled over engineers, who lorded it over everyone else. The motel owner's status depending on how successful he was an an entrepreneur. But then financial success was really at the root of the hierarchy among the doctors: surgeons - particularly thoracic surgeons - were treated as the maharajahs, everyone rising when this persona entered the room." Chapter 11, Page 205

"I was filled with a longing for home (whatever I conceived that to be) so strong that I sometimes wondered if I myself was dying and this feeling was a foreboding, the bittersweet messenger." Chapter 14, Page 229

"I liked to think of myself as nonjudgmental; I thought I didn't discriminate in my services: a game man with AIDS or a drug abuser would expect to be treated the same way as I would treat anyone else. But did I have a blind spot?" Chapter 15, Page 250

"My patients, by contrast, were in hiding. They were not inclined to a public demonstration of any sort, scared lest the tragedy of their HIV infection be compounded by the neighbors' knowledge of it." Chapter 17, Page 276

"My faith was vague, and not mediated by church or sect. In whatever way I saw God, I rarely saw him in the concrete terms Will was describing: a protector, an immediate presence." Chapter 17, Page 292

"On the playing field of medicine, with all its established positions and specialized players, I felt increasingly like the man from the moon, the man playing left-out. Nobody dwelled on what it was like to be in my shoes; they were merely thankful they were not." Chapter 20, Page 323

"I had always felt inexpert when a patient was near death. I knew I was not alone: the gallows humor evinced in comments like 'the patient is circling the drain,' or 'about to transfer to Central Office,' reflected the clumsy way all of us in the hospital dealt with impending death." Chapter 25, Page 363

"No matter how long I practice medicine, no matter what happens with this retrovirus, I will not be able to forget these young men, the little towns they came from, and the cruel, cruel irony of what awaited them in the big city." Chapter 28, Page 403

"The 'infection' dream is so frequent that many mornings I wake up and, even when I have shaved and showered, I am still having to convince myself that I am uninfected." Chapter 30, Page 415

Topics for Discussion

How does Abraham come to be interested in the field of infectious diseases? What happens that makes this field more desirable during the 1980s? Does Abraham seem happy in his choice? What makes you think so? Give an overview of Abraham's medical career up to and including his decision to leave Tennessee for Iowa.

How does Abraham come to be known locally as the "AIDS doctor?" What are the fears associated with the disease? How do these fears impact Abraham's personal life? How do they impact his professional life?

Who is Abraham's first patient with full-blown AIDS after his arrival in Tennessee? How does he come to know this young man? How is this patient treated throughout his illness? What is to be said about the character of this young man's home caregivers?

Who are Will and Bess Johnson? How do they come to be infected with AIDS? Abraham comes to question his own bias against the people who have contracted AIDS through unprotected sex. What role do Well and Bess play in this questioning? What is Will's attitude about faith? How does it change over the course of his illness?

Abraham says that he tries to call on various surgeons to provide operative procedures for AIDS patients. Why? There is an incident described about an AIDS patient's visit to the dentist. Recount that event and Abraham's involvement in it.

Who is Scotty Daws? Who is Ed Maupin? What do the two have in common? What is the general attitude of the nursing staff to the AIDS patients who are in the hospital? Are all nurses in agreement?

Abraham often feels that he is accomplishing nothing for the AIDS patients because he has not real treatment options. How does this change over the course of his term in Tennessee? Who is Raleigh? What is it that Abraham comes to believe about his duty to his patients after Raleigh's failed suicide attempt?

www.ingramcontent.com/pod-product-compliance
Ingram Content Group UK Ltd.
Pitfield, Milton Keynes, MK11 3LW, UK
UKHW041905190726
13854UKWH00003B/1100

9 781304 556691